KU-165-413

Great Meals in Minutes

Make-Ahead Menus

Great Meals in Minutes was created by Rebus Inc., and
published by Time-Life Books.

All rights reserved. No part of this publication may be
reproduced, stored in a retrieval system, or transmitted, in
any form or by any means, electronic, mechanical,
photocopying, recording or otherwise without the prior
permission of the copyright holder.

This edition published 1994 by Bloomsbury Books, an
imprint of The Godfrey Cave Group, 42 Bloomsbury Street,
London, WC1B 3QJ.

© 1994 Time-Life Books BV.

ISBN 1 85471 591 7

Printed and bound in Great Britain.

Make-Ahead Menus

Jenifer Harvey Lang

Menu 1

Brigand's Brochettes	8
Baked Brussels Sprouts	
Radish Salad	

Menu 2

Fish Schnitzel	10
Steamed Parslied Potatoes	
Red and Green Cabbage Salad	

Menu 3

Baked Fish with Pecan Stuffing	13
Cauliflower, Bell Pepper, and Olive Salad	

Marilyn Hansen

Menu 1

Beef Stroganoff with Kasha	18
Beetroot and Oranges Vinaigrette	

Menu 2

Bouillabaisse with Croutons and Rouille	20
Tomato-Chutney Aspic	

Menu 3

Swedish Meatballs	23
Cucumber and Radish Salad	

Margaret Fraser

Menu 1

Taramosalata with Crudités and Pitta Bread	28
Lamb Kebabs	
Stuffed Tomatoes	

Menu 2

Chilled Avgolemono	31
Spanakopita	
Marinated Artichokes with Greek Olives	

Menu 3

Moussaka	35
Lettuce with Cucumber-Yogurt Dressing	
Sesame Pitta Crisps/Melon with Ouzo Cream	

Roberta Rall

Menu 1

Spinach and Potato Soup	40
Salmon and Pasta Sunburst Salad with Herbed Mustard Sauce	

Menu 2

Seafood Provençal in Parchment	42
Lacy Potato Pancakes	
Honeydew-Avocado Salad	

Menu 3

Raclette Casseroles	46
Marinated Vegetable Salad	
Fruit in Filo Bundles	

Gloria Zimmerman

Menu 1

Thai Seafood Salad	52
Ginger Chicken	
White Rice	

Menu 2

Vietnamese Salad	54
Poached Chicken with Rice and Ginger Sauce	

Menu 3

Sour Beef Salad	58
Sweet Pork	
Broccoli with Oyster Sauce	

Bloomsbury Books
London

Cauliflower, Bell Pepper, and Olive Salad

Large head cauliflower (about 1 Kg (2 lb))
Small red bell pepper
Small green bell pepper
Small yellow bell pepper
10 extra-large pitted black olives
125 ml (4 fl oz) good-quality olive oil
1 tablespoon chopped parsley
1 tablespoon red or white wine vinegar
2 teaspoons Dijon mustard
2 flat anchovy fillets, or 2 teaspoons anchovy paste
Salt and freshly ground pepper
Large head lettuce

1 In large saucepan fitted with vegetable steamer, bring 2 1/2 cm (1 inch) water to a boil over high heat.
2 Meanwhile, wash and trim cauliflower and cut into florets. Place florets in steamer, cover pan, and cook 5 minutes.
3 While cauliflower cooks, wash and dry bell peppers. Halve, core, and seed peppers and cut lengthwise into thin strips; set aside.
4 Lift out steamer, reserving hot water in pan, and turn cauliflower into colander. Refresh under cold running water and set aside to drain.
5 Return water in pan to a boil. Replace steamer and add peppers. Cover pan and cook 1 minute. Meanwhile, drain olives and quarter lengthwise; place in large non-aluminium bowl.
6 Lift out steamer and turn peppers into large strainer; refresh peppers under cold running water and set aside to drain.
7 Meanwhile, for dressing combine olive oil, chopped parsley, vinegar, mustard, anchovies or anchovy paste, and salt and pepper to taste in blender. Blend about 15 seconds, or until emulsified.
8 Add cauliflower and peppers to olives in large non-aluminium bowl. Pour dressing over salad and toss well. Cover bowl with plastic wrap and refrigerate until 30 minutes before serving.
9 Thirty minutes before serving, remove salad from refrigerator. Toss salad and set aside to come to room temperature.
10 Wash lettuce and dry in salad spinner or with paper towels. Discard any bruised or discoloured leaves.
11 Place 2 or 3 large lettuce leaves on each dinner plate and top with salad.

Added touch
Hungary is famed for its pastries, and all Hungarian cooks have their own versions of this rich cottage cheese cake, known as *turós pite*. Meringue is piped on top in an appealing lattice pattern. Be sure to wash and dry the beaters and bowl after mixing the pastry dough; any trace of grease or egg yolk will keep the egg whites from beating up properly.

Latticed Cottage Cheese Cake

Pastry:
175 g (6 oz) plain flour
1/2 teaspoon baking soda
Pinch of salt
4 tablespoons unsalted butter, at room temperature
60 ml (2 fl oz) sour cream
60 g (2 oz) sugar
1 egg, at room temperature

Topping:
175 g (6 oz) cottage cheese
4 tablespoons sour cream
125 g (4 oz) plus 2 tablespoons sugar
1 egg yolk, at room temperature
1 tablespoon plain flour
1 teaspoon finely grated orange zest
30 g (1 oz) golden raisins
2 egg whites, at room temperature

1 Preheat oven to 190°C (375°F or Mark 5).
2 Prepare pastry: In large bowl, combine flour, baking soda, salt, butter, and sour cream. Beat with electric mixer about 1 minute, or until mixture resembles coarse cornmeal. Add sugar and egg and mix about 15 seconds, or just until dough forms a ball. Press dough into 22 1/2 cm (9 inch) square cake pan.
3 Bake pastry 20 minutes. Wash and dry beaters and bowl.
4 While pastry bakes, prepare topping: In food processor, combine cottage cheese, sour cream, 60 g (2 oz) sugar, the egg yolk, and orange zest. Process about 15 seconds, or until puréed. With rubber spatula, fold in raisins.
5 Place egg whites in large bowl and beat with electric mixer until frothy. Add remaining sugar and continue beating until soft peaks form.
6 After cake has baked 20 minutes, remove pan from oven and pour cottage cheese topping over cake. Fill pastry bag fitted with medium-size round tip with beaten egg whites and pipe meringue over topping in lattice pattern, making 4 strips in each direction. Or, spoon meringue onto topping in lattice patern.
7 Return cake to oven and bake an additional 15 minutes, or until topping is firm and meringue is browned. Let cake cool to room temperature and cut into squares to serve.

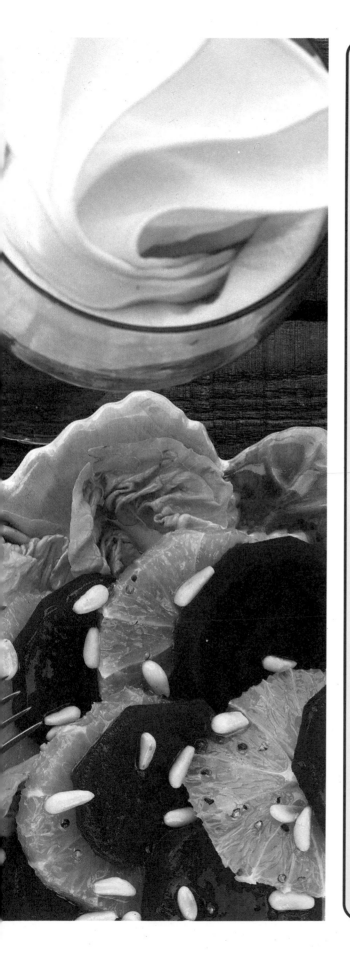

Marilyn Hansen

Menu 1
(left)
Beef Stroganoff with Kasha
Beetroot and Oranges Vinaigrette

Marilyn Hansen cites her extensive world travels as the major influence on her cooking. Wherever she visits, she makes a point of going to local restaurants and wineries and of collecting recipes from native cooks. When cooking at home, she often streamlines and lightens traditional recipes to save time and to suit diet-conscious friends. In the three menus she presents here, she gives new twists to classic international recipes.

The highlight of Menu 1 is the Russian favourite beef Stroganoff, sautéed strips or cubes of beef in a rich sour-cream-based sauce. Here Marilyn Hansen reduces calories by substituting low-fat yogurt for some of the sour cream. *Kasha*, or buckwheat groats, and dark pumpernickel bread are served with the Stroganoff.

Bouillabaisse is the main course of Menu 2, an ideal buffet meal. In this prepare-ahead version of the classic French seafood stew, the cook uses several kinds of fish as well as shrimp and mussels. For an original touch, she adds curry powder instead of the usual saffron threads. Tomato aspic, flavoured with lemon juice and chutney and presented on a bed of watercress, is the salad.

In the Scandinavian-inspired Menu 3, Marilyn Hansen gives traditional Swedish meatballs new zest with allspice and caraway seeds. She cooks the meatballs in advance, then reheats them in a creamy but not overly heavy gravy before serving. Marinated cucumbers with sliced radishes and radish sprouts are the colourful complement.

Everyone will welcome this substantial cold-weather dinner of beef Stroganoff served with kasha *and buttered black bread. The light salad of beetroot and oranges is sprinkled with pine nuts.*

Beef Stroganoff with Kasha
Beetroot and Oranges Vinaigrette

For a more dramatic presentation, serve the beef Stroganoff in a bread 'tureen.' Select a dense 500 g (1 lb) round loaf of dark pumpernickel bread and, using a serrated knife, cut off a lid about 5 cm (2 inches) from the top of the loaf. With a spoon, scoop out the interior of the loaf to form a bowl, leaving the walls about 1½–2½ cm (¾–1 inch) thick. Wrap the bowl and its lid in a plastic bag until serving time. Just before serving, place the bowl and lid on a cookie sheet in a preheated 180°C (350°F or Mark 4) oven to warm for 10 minutes. Spoon the *kasha* onto a large platter. Place the bread tureen on the bed of *kasha* and fill it with Stroganoff. To serve, spoon the Stroganoff onto individual dinner plates and cut the bread into wedges.

What to drink
The cook suggests a robust wine to match the earthy flavours of this menu. A California Zinfandel, Cabernet Sauvignon, or Merlot would be equally good.

Start-to-Finish Steps

The day before or the morning of serving
1 Follow Stroganoff recipe steps 1 and 2 and salad recipe steps 1 through 5.
2 Follow Stroganoff recipe steps 3 through 6.

Fifteen minutes before serving
1 Follow kasha recipe steps 1 through 3 and Stroganoff recipe steps 7 and 8.
2 While kasha and Stroganoff are cooking, follow salad recipe step 6.
3 Follow kasha recipe steps 4 and 5.
4 Follow Stroganoff recipe steps 9 and 10 and serve with salad.

Beef Stroganoff with Kasha

750 g (1½ lb) boneless top sirloin steak cut 2½ cm (1 inch) thick, or flank steak
Medium-size onion
Small bunch scallions
Medium-size clove garlic
250 g (8 oz) white mushrooms
Small bunch dill
30 g (1 oz) capers
125 g (4 oz) canned pitted black olives
6 tablespoons unsalted butter, approximately
2 tablespoons vegetable oil
500 ml (1 pt) sour cream
250 ml (8 fl oz) low-fat yogurt
1½ teaspoons salt
½ teaspoon freshly ground black pepper
1 tablespoon Worcestershire sauce
125 g (4 oz) chèvre
Large loaf dark pumpernickel bread
Kasha (see following recipe)

1 Wrap beef in plastic or foil and place in freezer at least 30 minutes, or until partially frozen.
2 Meanwhile, peel onion and halve lengthwise. Cut into thin wedges; set aside. Wash, dry, and trim scallions. Cut enough scallions, including green tops, diagonally into 1 cm (½ inch) slices to measure about 100 g (3 oz). Peel and crush garlic. Wipe mushrooms clean with damp paper towels and slice thinly. Wash dill and pat dry. Wrap and refrigerate 4 sprigs for garnish and finely chop enough remaining dill to measure 30 g (1 oz). Drain capers. Drain olives and thinly slice.
3 When beef is firm, cut across grain into thin slices. Cut slices into 1 x 5 cm (½ x 2 inch) long strips.
4 In large deep heavy-gauge skillet, melt 1 tablespoon butter in 1 tablespoon oil over medium-high heat. Add one third of beef strips and sauté, stirring, about 2 minutes, or until browned. Using slotted spatula, transfer cooked beef to medium-size bowl. Sauté remaining beef in two batches and add to bowl.
5 Add onion to skillet and sauté, stirring, 2 minutes, or until slightly wilted; add to bowl with beef. Add remaining 1 tablespoon oil and 1 tablespoon butter to skillet along with scallions, garlic, and mushrooms, and sauté, stirring, 1 minute; add to beef.

6 Add sour cream, yogurt, chopped dill, salt, and pepper to skillet and cook, stirring, 2 minutes, or until almost boiling. (Do not allow mixture to boil.) Add Worcestershire sauce, capers, olives, and beef-onion mixture, and stir to blend. Return mixture to bowl, cover, and refrigerate until about 15 minutes before serving.

7 About 15 minutes before serving, turn Stroganoff into large heavy-gauge skillet and cook, stirring occasionally, 7 to 10 minutes, or until heated through. Do not allow Stroganoff to boil.

8 Meanwhile, cut chèvre into small cubes; set aside. Slice bread, and butter generously.

9 When Stroganoff is hot, stir in chèvre and mix gently; chèvre does not have to melt completely.

10 To serve, divide kasha among 4 dinner plates. Spoon Stroganoff over kasha and garnish with dill sprigs. Serve with buttered bread.

Kasha

750 ml (1½ pts) beef stock
125 g (4 oz) medium or coarse kasha
1 egg
¾ teaspoon salt
¼ teaspoon freshly ground black pepper
Small bunch parsley
2 tablespoon unsalted butter

1 In medium-size saucepan, bring beef stock to a boil over high heat.

2 Meanwhile, combine kasha, egg, salt, and pepper in large heavy-gauge saucepan over low heat. Mix well and stir until kasha is dry.

3 When stock boils, add it to kasha mixture and cover pan. Reduce heat to medium-low and cook, stirring with fork once or twice, 7 to 10 minutes, or until kasha grains are tender.

4 Wash and dry parsley. Finely chop enough parsley to measure 15 g (½ oz).

5 Add parsley and butter to kasha, tossing with fork to combine. Cover and keep warm on stove top until ready to serve.

Beetroot and Oranges Vinaigrette

6 medium-size fresh beetroot (about 500 g (1 lb) total weight)
2 medium-size navel oranges or blood oranges
60 g (2 oz) pine nuts
100 ml (3 fl oz) vegetable oil
3 tablespoons white wine vinegar
2 teaspoons honey
1 teaspoon Dijon mustard
¼ teaspoon salt
¼ teaspoon freshly ground pepper
Large head lettuce or large bunch watercress

1 Bring 2½ cm (1 inch) of water to a boil in large heavy-gauge saucepan. Meanwhile, wash beetroot, being careful not to damage skin. Trim beetroot tops, leaving 2½ cm (1 inch) of tops attached. Place beetroot in vegetable steamer over boiling water, cover pan, and steam 15 to 20 minutes, or until tender.

2 Meanwhile, peel oranges, removing all white pith. Slice oranges crosswise into 5 mm (¼ inch) slices, place in plastic bag, and refrigerate until ready to serve.

3 In small dry skillet, toast pine nuts over medium heat, stirring, about 2 minutes, or until lightly browned. Remove pan from heat; add oil, vinegar, honey, mustard, salt, and pepper, and stir to blend. Pour dressing into jar with tight-fitting lid and refrigerate until needed.

4 When beetroot is cooked, turn into colander and cool under cold running water; drain well. Slip off skins and cut into 5 mm (¼ inch) slices. Place beetroot in plastic bag and refrigerate until needed.

5 Wash lettuce or watercress and dry in salad spinner or with paper towels. Wrap in dry paper towels, place in plastic bag, and refrigerate until needed.

6 Just before serving, make a bed of lettuce or watercress on each of 4 salad plates. Arrange beetroot and orange slices on greens. Shake salad dressing well to recombine, and drizzle some dressing over each salad.

The popular Greek appetizer taramosalata, known as 'poor man's caviar,' is a creamy purée most often served as a dip or spread. It is usually made from the tiny orange eggs, or roe (tarama), of carp, although occasionaly tuna or gray mullet roe is used. Look for tarama in bottles in Greek and Middle Eastern markets or in speciality food shops. If you are on a salt-restricted diet, soak the tarama in water for 5 to 10 minutes, then drain it well. Tarama keps in the refrigerator for up to three months; taramosalata can be made up to five days in advance of serving and stored in the refrigerator.

What to drink

A Cabernet Sauvignon is always a good choice with lamb. Try a young California Cabernet or one from the Médoc region.

Start-to-Finish Steps

The day before or the morning of serving
1 Wash 2 lemons and dry with paper towels. Halve lemons. Cut 3 thick slices from one half for kebabs recipe. Squeeze enough juice from remaining halves to measure 1/4 cup for taramosalata recipe. Crush and peel 4 cloves garlic for kebabs recipe. Peel and mince remaining clove for stuffed tomatoes recipe.
2 Follow stuffed tomatoes recipe step 1.
3 Follow kebabs recipe steps 1 and 2.
4 Follow stuffed tomatoes recipe steps 2 through 8.
5 While tomatoes are baking, follow taramosalata recipe steps 1 through 4.

Thirty minutes before serving
1 Follow kebabs recipe step 3, stuffed tomatoes recipe step 9, and taramosalata recipe step 5.
2 Follow kebabs recipe steps 4 through 6.
3 While kebabs are broiling, follow taramosalata recipe steps 6 through 9.
4 Follow stuffed tomatoes recipe step 10, kebabs recipe step 7, and serve with taramosalata.

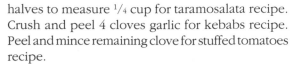

Taramosalata with Crudités and Pitta Bread

3 thick slices home-style white bread
Small onion
100 g (3 oz) tarama
4 tablespoons lemon juice
1/2 teaspoon salt
Freshly ground pepper
125 ml (4 fl oz) good-quality olive oil
Large courgette
Large red bell pepper
Two 10 cm (6 inch) pitta breads

1 Place white bread on plate, pour 175 ml (6 fl oz) water over bread, and let soak 10 minutes.
2 Meanwhile, peel and coarsely chop onion. In food processor or blender, combine onion, tarama, lemon juice, salt, and pepper to taste. Process until combined.
3 Gently squeeze out excess water from bread and tear bread into chunks. Add to food processor or blender and process until smooth.
4 With machine running, add olive oil in a slow, steady stream. Process until mixture is smooth and light pink in colour. Transfer to small serving

bowl, cover, and refrigerate until 30 minutes before serving.

5 Thirty minutes before serving, set out taramosalata to come to room temperature.

6 Wash courgette and bell pepper and dry with paper towels. Trim courgette and cut crosswise into 5 mm (¼ inch) slices. Core and seed bell pepper; cut into 2½ cm (1 inch) squares.

7 Cut each pitta bread into 6 wedges.

8 Five minutes before serving, wrap pitta wedges in foil and warm in broiler or very hot oven 2 to 3 minutes. Place in napkin-lined basket to keep warm.

9 Divide courgette slices and bell pepper squares among 4 salad plates and serve with taramosalata and pitta.

Lamb Kebabs

Small bunch fresh rosemary, or 2 teaspoons dried
3 thick slices lemon, plus 1 lemon for garnish
4 medium-size cloves garlic, crushed and peeled
125 ml (4 fl oz) good-quality olive oil

Salt and freshly ground pepper
850 g (1¾ lb) lean boneless lamb, cut into 2½ cm (1 inch) cubes

1 Wash fresh rosemary, if using, and pat dry with paper towels. Reserve 4 sprigs for garnish. Mince enough remaining rosemary to measure 2 tablespoons.

2 Combine lemon slices, fresh or dried rosemary, garlic, olive oil, and salt and pepper to taste in shallow glass or ceramic dish. Add lamb, cover with plastic wrap, and refrigerate, turning lamb occasionally, at least 2 hours or overnight.

3 Thirty minutes before serving, preheat broiler. Remove lamb from refrigerator.

4 Wash and dry lemon for garnish. Cut into 12 wedges; set aside.

5 Remove lamb from marinade and thread onto four 25–30 cm (10–12 inch) skewers. Arrange skewers in broiler pan.

6 Broil kebabs about 10 cm (6 inches) from heat, turning occasionally and brushing generously with marinade, 12 minutes, or until browned.

7 Transfer kebabs to dinner plates and garnish with lemon wedges, and rosemary sprigs if desired.

Stuffed Tomatoes

4 medium-size tomatoes (about 750 g (1½ lb) total weight)
Salt
60 g (2 oz) long-grain white rice
2 tablespoons pine nuts
2 tablespoons good-quality olive oil
Medium-size clove garlic, minced
¼ teaspoon dried thyme
¼ teaspoon dried oregano
Small bunch chives for garnish (optional)

1 Preheat oven to 190°C (375°F or Mark 5). Lightly grease shallow 1-quart baking dish.
2 Bring 175 ml (6 fl oz) water to a boil over high heat in small saucepan.
3 Wash tomatoes and dry with paper towels. Cut tops off tomatoes. Scoop out and reserve pulp; remove and discard seeds. Lightly salt insides of tomato shells and invert on paper towels to drain.
4 Add rice to boiling water, cover, and cook over medium-low heat 20 minutes, or until tender.
5 Meanwhile, brown pine nuts in small dry skillet over medium heat 3 to 4 minutes, stirring constantly. Transfer pine nuts to small bowl and set aside.
6 Heat oil in skillet over medium heat until hot. Add garlic, thyme, oregano, and reserved tomato pulp and cook 3 to 4 minutes, or until excess liquid has evaporated. Remove skillet from heat and stir in rice and pine nuts.
7 Place tomato shells in prepared baking dish and spoon stuffing into shells.
8 Bake tomatoes 15 to 20 minutes, or until stuffing is lightly browned. Let tomatoes cool slightly, then cover and refrigerate until 30 minutes before serving.
9 Thirty minutes before serving, remove tomatoes from refrigerator to come to room temperature. Wash chives, if using, and dry with paper towels. Mince enough chives to measure 1 tablespoon; reserve remainder for another use.
10 Sprinkle tomatoes with chives, if desired, and transfer to dinner plates.

Chilled Avgolemono
Spanakopita
Marinated Artichokes with Greek Olives

Offer the delicate lemon and egg soup before or with the spanakopita *and the salad of marinated artichokes and olives.*

The spinach and feta cheese filling for the spanakopita is wrapped in filo, tissue-thin pastry sheets that are sold frozen. To prevent the sheet from cracking when you separate them, thaw the entire block of frozen filo in the refrigerator overnight. Never refreeze the extra dough or the sheets may stick together; refrigerate it and use it within a week.

Because filo becomes crumbly when exposed to air, work quickly and have your other ingredients ready before unrolling the dough. Unroll the dough and place eight sheets, unseparated, on a damp kitchen towel covered with plastic wrap; cover the top sheet with another piece of plastic wrap and a second damp towel. Work with one sheet of dough at a time, leaving the rest covered. The butter you brush on the sheets helps to separate the layers and turn the pastry a golden brown as it bakes. But take care – too much butter will make the pastry soggy. If feta cheese is unavailable, substitute a creamy chèvre or plain cream cheese. The flavour of the finished dish will not be as tangy, but it will still be good.

What to drink

A crisp, dry, flavourful white wine, such as a French Sancerre or a Sauvignon Blanc from California or Italy, goes best with these dishes.

Start-to-Finish Steps

The morning of serving
1 Wash 2 lemons and dry with paper towels. Halve 1 lemon for artichokes recipe. Squeeze enough

juice from remaining lemon to measure $1/3$ cup and set aside for avgolemono recipe.
2 Follow spanakopita recipe steps 1 and 2.
3 Follow avgolemono recipe steps 1 and 2 and artichokes recipe steps 1 through 3.
4 Follow avgolemono recipe step 3.
5 While rice is cooking, follow artichokes recipe step 4 and spanakopita recipe step 3.
6 Follow avgolemono recipe step 4 and spanakopita recipe step 4.
7 Follow artichokes recipe steps 5 and 6.
8 Follow spanakopita recipe steps 5 through 10.

About thirty minutes before serving
1 Follow spanakopita recipe steps 11 and 12.
2 Toward end of spanakopita baking time, follow artichokes recipe steps 7 and 8 and avgolemono recipe steps 5 and 6.
3 Follow spanakopita recipe step 13 and serve with avgolemono and artichokes.

Chilled Avgolemono

1 ltr ($1^3/_4$ pts) chicken stock
Small bunch mint
60 g (2 oz) long-grain white rice
2 eggs
100 ml (3 fl oz) lemon juice
Salt and freshly ground white pepper
Large lemon for garnish

1 Bring stock to a boil in medium-size saucepan over high heat.
2 Meanwhile, wash mint and pat dry with paper towels. Enclose 4 sprigs mint in small square of cheesecloth and tie securely with kitchen string. Wrap remaining mint in plastic and reserve.
3 Add cheesecloth packet and rice to stock. Reduce heat to medium-low, cover, and cook 15 to 20 minutes, or until rice is tender. Discard cheesecloth packet.
4 In large non-aluminium bowl, beat eggs with whisk until light and frothy. Add hot stock and rice very slowly, whisking constantly. (If stock is added too quickly, eggs will curdle.) Stir in lemon juice, and salt and pepper to taste. Cover bowl with plastic wrap and refrigerate until just before serving.
5 Just before serving, wash lemon and dry with paper towel. Cut 4 thin slices for garnish. Finely chop enough reserved mint to measure 1 teaspoon.
6 Divide soup among 4 bowls and garnish each with a lemon slice and some chopped mint.

Spanakopita

Small bunch dill
125 g (4 oz) fresh mushrooms
Medium-size onion
500 g (1 lb) spinach
7 tablespoons unsalted butter
3 eggs
250 g (8 oz) feta cheese
1/2 teaspoon each dried oregano and thyme
1/2 teaspoon salt
8 sheets frozen filo dough, thawed

1   Wash dill and pat dry with paper towels. Finely chop enough dill to measure 2 tablespoons. Wipe mushrooms clean with damp paper towels and chop finely. Peel and finely chop onion.

2   Wash spinach in several changes of cold water. Do not dry. Remove tough stems and discard.

3   Place spinach in large saucepan and cook, covered, over medium-high heat 3 to 5 minutes, or until just wilted. Turn spinach into colander and refresh under cold running water. Drain well, pressing out excess moisture with back of spoon. Finely chop spinach; set aside.

4   Melt 2 tablespoons butter in large skillet over medium heat. Add onion and mushrooms and cook 3 minutes, or until soft. Remove from heat and add spinach; stir to combine and allow to cool 10 minutes.

5   Beat eggs lightly in small bowl and add to spinach mixture. Crumble in feta and add chopped dill, oregano, thyme, and salt. Set aside.

6   Melt remaining 5 tablespoons butter in small saucepan.

7   Butter bottom and sides of 20 cm (8 inch) square baking pan. Brush 1 sheet of filo lightly on one side with melted butter. Fold sheet to 20 cm (8 inch) width so that when placed in pan it completely covers bottom and overhangs evenly on two opposite sides.

8   Rotate pan a quarter turn and repeat procedure with another sheet of buttered filo. Repeat with 4 more sheets of filo, rotating pan a quarter turn each time. (Filo should hang over edges of pan on all four sides.)

9   Spread spinach-cheese filling over filo, smoothing top. One side at a time, fold overhanging filo over filling.

10 Cut remaining 2 sheets of filo into four 20 cm (8 inch) squares. Layer squares on top of filled pastry, brushing each square with melted butter before placing the next on top. Score top of spanakopita with sharp paring knife just through pastry layers (dividing it into 4 quarters) to ensure neat portions after baking. Cover with plastic wrap and refrigerate until 30 minutes before serving.

11 About 30 minutes before serving, preheat oven to 190°C (375°F or Mark 5).

12 Bake spanakopita 30 minutes, or until golden brown.

13 Cut spanakopita into four pieces and transfer to dinner plates.

Marinated Artichokes with Greek Olives

8 to 10 fresh baby artichokes (about 350 g (12 oz) total weight), or two large cans water-packed artichoke hearts
Small bunch fresh rosemary, or 1 teaspoon dried
Large lemon, halved
125 ml (4 fl oz) good-quality olive oil
Freshly ground black pepper
125 g (4 oz) small Greek olives

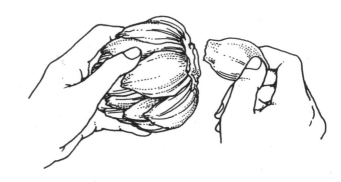

1 Bring 750 ml (1¹/₂ pts) water to a boil in medium-size saucepan.
2 Meanwhile, wash fresh artichokes and fresh rosemary, if using, and pat dry with paper towels. Roughly chop enough rosemary to measure 1 tablespoon and reserve remaining rosemary for another use. Pull off and discard any discoloured leaves from artichokes and trim stems. Using kitchen scissors, cut off tips of remaining leaves and rub cut surfaces with 1 lemon half.
3 If using canned artichokes, rinse and drain in colander, and sprinkle with juice from lemon half, if desired.
4 Add used lemon half and fresh artichokes to boiling water. Cover pan and simmer gently over medium-low heat 15 minutes, or until artichokes are tender when stems are pierced with a fork.
5 Combine olive oil, fresh or dried rosemary, and pepper to taste in large non-aluminium bowl. Cut remaining lemon half into 3 or 4 slices and add to bowl.
6 Drain fresh artichokes in colander and halve lengthwise. Add fresh or canned artichokes to marinade, cover bowl with plastic wrap, and refrigerate until 30 minutes before serving, stirring occasionally.
7 Just before serving, drain olives in strainer.
8 Using slotted spoon, transfer artichokes to salad plates. Divide olives among plates and serve.

Honeydew-Avocado Salad

Large shallot
30 g (1 oz) hazelnuts or walnuts
Small avocado
4 tablespoons vegetable oil
2 tablespoons hazelnut or walnut oil
2½ tablespoons lime juice
1 teaspoon Dijon mustard
⅛ teaspoon salt
⅛ teaspoon freshly ground black pepper
Small head lettuce
Medium-size head Belgian endive
Small honeydew melon

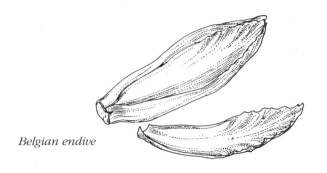

Belgian endive

1 Peel and mince shallot; set aside.
2 If using hazelnuts, place on baking sheet and toast in 220°C (425°F or Mark 7) oven, stirring occasionally, 5 to 7 minutes, or until skins split.
3 Meanwhile, halve and pit avocado. Peel halves and cut into 1 cm (½ inch) slices.
4 Combine shallots, oils, lime juice, mustard, salt, and pepper in small non-aluminium bowl and whisk to blend. Add avocado slices and turn to coat with dressing. Set aside.
5 Remove hazelnuts from oven and set aside to cool.
6 Wash lettuce; discard any bruised or discoloured leaves. Trim endive and separate leaves. Dry lettuce and endive in salad spinner or with paper towels; set aside.
7 Halve and seed honeydew. Using melon baller, cut enough fruit into balls to measure about 350 g (12 oz). Reserve remaining melon for another use.
8 Place hazelnuts in kitchen towel and rub between hands to remove skins. Coarsely chop hazelnuts or walnuts.
9 Line 4 salad plates with lettuce. Arrange endive, avocado, and melon balls decoratively on lettuce. Stir dressing and drizzle over salads. Sprinkle with nuts and serve.

<table>
<tr>
<td>

Menu

3

</td>
<td>

Raclette Casseroles
Marinated Vegetable Salad
Fruit in Filo Bundles

</td>
</tr>
</table>

Raclette (from the French verb racler, 'to scrape') is best if you use authentic Swiss raclette cheese, which has a firm texture and a mild nutty taste. If it is unavailable, substitute another mild, easy-melting cheese such as Swiss, Jarlsberg, or Gruyère.

The fruit-filled filo bundles are perfect for make-ahead meals because they can be prepared up to 24 hours in advance and held in the refrigerator until you are ready to bake them. Vary the fruit filling according to the season; for example, you can use fresh peaches instead of the pears and apples.

What to drink

A full-bodied white California Chardonnay or good French Chablis would be an excellent selection here.

Start-to-Finish Steps

The morning of serving

1 Wash lemon. Grate enough rind to measure 1 teaspoon each for salad and filo bundles recipes. Halve lemon; squeeze enough juice to measure 1 tablespoon for salad recipe.

Piping hot raclette *casseroles, a vegetable salad with sugar snap peas, and fruit-filled filo for dessert make an elegant supper.*

2 Follow filo bundles recipe steps 1 through 7.
3 Follow salad recipe steps 1 through 9.
4 Follow raclette recipe steps 1 through 7.

Thirty minutes before serving
1 Follow raclette recipe steps 8 through 12.
2 Follow salad recipe steps 10 and 11.
3 Follow raclette recipe step 13, filo bundles recipe step 8, and serve raclette casseroles with salad.
4 Follow filo bundles recipe step 9 and serve for dessert.

Raclette Casseroles

750 g (1¹/₂ lb) small new red potatoes
350 g (12 oz) Black Forest ham, in one piece
Salt
Small bunch broccoli (about 500 g (1 lb))
250 g (8 oz) raclette cheese
2 tablespoons unsalted butter
2 tablespoons plain flour
300 ml (10 fl oz) milk
¹/₈ teaspoon freshly ground black pepper
Pinch of nutmeg

1 Bring 2¹/₂ ltrs (4 pts) water to a boil in large saucepan over high heat.
2 Meanwhile, scrub and dry potatoes and cut into 1 cm (¹/₂ inch) thick slices. Cut ham into 2¹/₂ cm (1 inch) cubes; set aside.
3 Add ¹/₂ teaspoon salt and potatoes to boiling water. Boil, stirring occasionally, 8 minutes.
4 Meanwhile, wash and dry broccoli. Cut broccoli tops into florets. Reserve stems for another use.
5 When potatoes have cooked 8 minutes, add broccoli, reduce heat to medium-low, and simmer 5 minutes, or until potatoes and broccoli are tender.
6 Turn vegetables into colander to drain and cool.
7 When cooled, place potatoes, broccoli, and ham in plastic bag. Close bag tightly and refrigerate until 30 minutes before serving.
8 Thirty minutes before serving, preheat oven to 200°C (400°F or Mark 6). Grease 4 individual heatproof casseroles.
9 Cut enough cheese into 2¹/₂ cm (1 inch) cubes to measure 2 cups. Cut remaining cheese into thin strips and set aside.
10 Melt butter over medium heat in small saucepan. Stir in flour, then gradually add milk. Stirring constantly, cook 1 minute, or until smooth. Add ¹/₄ teaspoon salt, pepper, and nutmeg and continue to cook over medium heat, stirring occasionally, 3 to 4 minutes, or until mixture comes just to a boil. Remove from heat and stir in cheese cubes.
11 Divide half of potatoes, broccoli, and ham among individual casseroles. Spoon 60 ml (2 fl oz) sauce into each casserole and top with remaining vegetables and ham. Spoon remaining sauce over top.
12 Bake raclettes 15 minutes.
13 Top raclettes with reserved cheese strips and bake another 5 minutes, or until bubbling.

Marinated Vegetable Salad

250 g (8 oz) sugar snap peas or green beans
6 radishes
Small red onion
2 eggs
125 g (4 oz) fresh mushrooms
1 tablespoon lemon juice
1 teaspoon grated lemon rind
1 teaspoon Dijon mustard
$^1/_2$ teaspoon salt
$^1/_8$ teaspoon freshly ground black pepper
125 ml (4 fl oz) vegetable oil
Small head lettuce

1 Wash, dry, and trim peas or beans and radishes. If using beans, cut into $7^1/_2$ cm (3 inch) lengths. Thinly slice radishes. Peel and thinly slice onion. Place radishes and onion in large non-aluminium bowl.
2 Separate eggs, placing yolks in small bowl and reserving whites for another use.
3 Bring $2^1/_2$ cm (1 inch) water to a boil in medium-size saucepan fitted with vegetable steamer.
4 Meanwhile, wipe mushrooms clean with damp paper towel and cut into 5 mm ($^1/_4$ inch) slices. Add to bowl with radishes and onion.
5 Place peas or beans in steamer, cover pan, and steam 3 minutes.
6 Meanwhile, in food processor or blender, combine egg yolks, lemon juice, lemon rind, mustard, salt, and pepper. Process 10 seconds, or until combined. With machine running, add oil in a slow, steady stream.
7 Transfer peas or beans to colander, refresh under cold running water, and allow to drain.
8 Add peas or beans to large bowl.
9 Drizzle dressing over vegetables, toss to combine, cover, and refrigerate until just before serving.
10 To serve, wash lettuce and dry with paper towels. Discard any bruised or discoloured leaves. Line salad bowl with lettuce leaves.
11 Gently toss marinated vegetables and add to salad bowl.

Fruit in Filo Bundles

175 g (6 oz) unsalted butter
2 large pears (about 500 g (1 lb) total weight)
Large Granny Smith apple
125 g (4 oz) plus 2 teaspoons sugar
30 g (1 oz) dark raisins
2 tablespoons plain flour
1 teaspoon grated lemon rind
$^3/_4$ teaspoon cinnamon
$^1/_8$ teaspoon nutmeg
16 sheets filo, thawed

1 Lightly grease baking sheet. Melt butter in small saucepan over medium-low heat.
2 Peel pears and apple. Core fruit and cut into wedges, then cut crosswise into very thin slices.
3 Combine 125 g (4 oz) sugar, raisins, flour, lemon rind, $^1/_2$ teaspoon cinnamon, and nutmeg in medium-size bowl.
4 Add fruit and toss to coat well.
5 Place filo sheets on a damp towel covered with plastic wrap and cover top sheet with plastic wrap and a second damp towel. To make one bundle, lay 1 sheet flat on work surface and brush lightly with melted butter. Top with second sheet and brush lightly with butter. Repeat procedure with

third sheet. Fold fourth sheet in half and centre on stack. Brush lightly with butter and spoon one fourth of fruit filling onto centre of folded sheet.

6   Fold over long sides of filo to cover fruit. Fold over short sides, twisting edges in centre to close bundle. Brush with butter and transfer to prepared baking sheet. Make 3 more bundles in same manner.

7   Combine remaining 2 teaspoons sugar and $^1/_4$ teaspoon cinnamon in small bowl. Sprinkle over bundles, cover pan, and refrigerate until 30 minutes before serving.

8   To bake, place bundles in 200°C (400°F or Mark 6) oven for 25 minutes, or until golden brown.

9   Using wire metal spatula, transfer filo bundles to napkin-lined platter, and serve hot.

Added touch

These ultra-crisp breadsticks made with pumpernickel rye flour can be topped with coarse salt or caraway seeds before baking. Or try fennel or anise seeds.

Pumpernickel Breadsticks

150 g (5 oz) plain flour, approximately
125 g (4 oz) pumpernickel rye flour, or regular rye flour
1 packet 7$^1/_2$ g ($^1/_4$ oz) fast-acting yeast
1 tablespoon brown sugar
1 tablespoon unsweetened cocoa powder
1 teaspoon salt
4 tablespoons vegetable oil
1 tablespoon molasses
30 g (1 oz) cornmeal
1 egg white
Coarse salt or caraway seeds

1   In food processor fitted with dough blade, combine flours, yeast, sugar, cocoa, and salt. Process 10 seconds, or until combined. With machine running, gradually add 60 ml (2 fl oz) hot tap water. Or, combine ingredients in large bowl and stir with wooden spoon.

2   Combine 125 ml (4 fl oz) cold water, oil, and molasses in small bowl. With processor running, gradually add mixture and process until dough forms a ball. Or, add molasses mixture to large bowl and stir with wooden spoon. (Dough will be quite sticky. If it is too sticky to handle, add 1 tablespoon flour. If it is too dry, add 1 teaspoon water.)

3   Process or stir 1 minute more to knead dough. Let dough rest 20 minutes. Meanwhile, sprinkle two large baking sheets with cornmeal.

4   Transfer dough to lightly floured surface. Halve dough and cut each half into 16 pieces. Roll each piece into a 17$^1/_2$ cm (7 inch) stick. Arrange sticks 2$^1/_2$ cm (1 inch) apart on baking sheets. Cover sheets with kitchen towels and let rise in warm place 30 minutes.

5   Preheat oven to 180°C (350°F or Mark 4).

6   Lightly beat egg white with 1 teaspoon water in small bowl. Brush breadsticks with egg white and sprinkle with coarse salt or caraway seeds. Bake 30 minutes, or until crisp. Transfer to rack to cool.

Gloria Zimmerman

Menu 1
(left)
Thai Seafood Soup
Ginger Chicken
White Rice

When Gloria Zimmerman was learning to cook Thai and Vietnamese dishes, she needed a teacher to explain the ingredients to her and a translator to help her order them in the ethnic markets, where no one spoke English. Today, to her delight, many more sources offer the exotic ingredients required by these two cuisines. Here she presents two Thai menus and one from Vietnam, all featuring intriguing combinations of colours and flavours – and all suited for make-ahead meals. Although Gloria Zimmerman suggests alternatives for those ingredients that may be hard to get, she strongly recommends using ethnic products to achieve authentic results.

In Menu 1, she prepares a Thai seafood soup called *po taek*. This rich combination of shrimp, fish, mussels, and squid is flavoured with lemon grass and other Thai seasonings and is followed by a main course of chicken cooked with ginger.

A Vietnamese meal, Menu 2 begins with a salad of pork, whole shrimp, and egg strips served over bean sprouts and marinated onions. Although the salad might seem like a meal in itself, in Vietnam it is typically followed by a meat course. Here the cook offers poached chicken bathed in a spicy ginger-garlic sauce.

In Menu 3, the steak for the Thai sour beef salad is broiled early on the day of serving, then, just before dinnertime, sliced and flavoured with fish sauce, lime juice, and hot red or green chili peppers if desired. Sweetened pork slices and broccoli with oyster sauce provide interesting flavour contrasts to the beef. You can also serve rice with this meal.

The Thai seafood soup is a beautiful mix of tastes and textures. As additional seasonings, offer lime juice, fish sauce, and red pepper flakes on the side. Present the ginger chicken and rice after the soup.

<table>
<tr><td>

Menu

1
</td><td>

Thai Seafood Soup
Ginger Chicken
White Rice
</td></tr>
</table>

The seafood soup contains a number of ingredients used frequently in Thai cooking, among them lemon grass, dried *galangal* (also known as *kha*), and dried keffir lime leaves (*makrut*). Lemon grass is a tall woody grass resembling a large scallion, with an intriguing sour taste. Sometimes available fresh, but more often dried, lemon grass is sold in Asian groceries. If you buy fresh, use only the portion of the stalk up the point where the grey-green leaves begin to branch off. If you use dried lemon grass, wrap it in cheesecloth for cooking and discard it before serving. An acceptable substitute is the rind from half a lemon.

Galangal (or *galingale*) is a rhizome, like ginger, but with a more delicate taste. Dried *galangal* is inexpensive and can be bought at Thai groceries. If it is unavailable, substitute a 1 cm (1/2 inch) piece of ginger. The lime leaves come from the keffir lime tree. Most Oriental markets sell the leaves dried; Thai groceries often stock them frozen. As an alternative, you can use fresh lemon or lime leaves or the rind from half a lime.

The chicken dish gains an interesting texture with the addition of tree ear (also known as cloud ear) mushrooms. Sold dried, these fairly bland mushrooms expand to five or six times their original size when soaked. If they are unavailable, omit them from the recipe.

What to drink
Dark, full-bodied beer, served ice cold, is the best beverage for these spicy dishes. Try a Japanese or Mexican brand.

Start-to-Finish Steps

The day before or morning of serving
1 Follow chicken recipe step 1 and soup recipe steps 1 through 3.
2 Follow chicken recipe steps 2 through 5.
3 Follow soup recipe steps 4 through 7.

*Thirty minutes before serving*1   Follow soup recipe step 8 and rice recipe steps 1 and 2.
2 While rice is cooking, follow soup recipe steps 9 through 12 and serve as first course.
3 Follow chicken recipe step 6, rice recipe step 3, and serve.

Thai Seafood Soup

2 stalks fresh or dried lemon grass, cut into 5 cm (2 inch) sections, or rind of 1/2 lemon
500 g (1 lb) can straw mushrooms
6 slices dried galangal, or 1 cm (1/2 inch) piece fresh ginger, peeled and thinly sliced
5 dried keffir lime leaves, or rind of 1/2 lime
500 g (1 lb) mussels, or 250 g (8 oz) crabmeat
250 g (8 oz) medium-size shrimp
250 g (8 oz) squid, cleaned
350 g (12 oz) haddock, sole, or flounder fillets, preferably with skin
3 large limes
175 ml (6 fl oz) Thai fish sauce (nam pla) or soy sauce
Red pepper flakes (optional)

1 Bring 1 1/2 ltrs (2 1/2 pts) water to a boil in large saucepan over high heat.
2 Meanwhile, wrap dried lemon grass, if using, in piece of cheesecloth and tie securely with kitchen string. Drain mushrooms in colander.
3 Add lemon grass or lemon rind, straw mushrooms, galangal or sliced ginger, and lime leaves or lime rind to boiling water. Boil 5 minutes, or until stock becomes aromatic. Remove pan from heat and, when stock has cooled cover and refrigerate until 30 minutes before serving.
4 Scrub mussels, if using, and remove hairlike beards. Rinse mussels and place in large bowl. Cover, and refrigerate until 30 minutes before serving.
5 Peel and devein shrimp, leaving tails intact. Place shrimp in medium-size bowl, cover, and refrigerate until 30 minutes before serving.
6 Separate squid tentacles from body sac. Cut body sac open lengthwise and lay flat, fleshier side up. Without cutting through flesh completely, score diagonally in both directions. If squid is large, halve lengthwise. Wrap in plastic and refrigerate until 30 minutes before serving.
7 Wipe fish fillets with damp paper towels. Cut fillets into 5 x 2 1/2 cm (2 x 1 inch) pieces. Wrap in plastic and refrigerate until 30 minutes before serving.
8 Thirty minutes before serving, bring stock to a simmer over medium heat.
9 Add squid and return soup to a simmer. Add mussels or crabmeat and return soup to a simmer.

Add pieces of fish and return soup to a simmer.

10 Skim froth from soup. Cover pan and simmer 2 minutes, or until seafood is completely cooked. Discard any unopened mussels. Meanwhile, halve and juice limes.

11 Add 3 tablespoons fish sauce or soy sauce and 4 tablespoons lime juice to soup and stir. Place remaining fish sauce, remaining lime juice, and red pepper flakes if using in small bows to serve as condiments.

12 Ladle soup into large serving bowl or tureen or into 4 individual soup bowls and serve with condiments.

Ginger Chicken

2 tablespoons dried tree ear mushrooms (optional)
500 g (1 lb) boneless, skinless chicken breasts
Medium-size clove garlic
5 cm (2 inch) piece fresh ginger
2 tablespoons vegetable oil
2 teaspoons sugar
2 tablespoons dark soy sauce

1 If using mushrooms, place in small bowl, add hot water to cover, and let soak 20 minutes.

2 Cut chicken into 2¹/₂ cm (1 inch) pieces. Peel and mince garlic. Peel ginger and cut lengthwise into thin strips.

3 Drain mushrooms in strainer; discard liquid. Rinse mushrooms well and pat dry with paper towels.

4 Heat oil in wok or large heavy-gauge skillet over medium heat until hot. Add garlic and stir-fry 30 seconds, or until golden brown. Add chicken and stir-fry 3 minutes, or until flesh is opaque.

5 Add ginger and stir-fry 1 minute. Add mushrooms, if using, and stir well. Stir in sugar and soy sauce and remove wok or skillet from heat. When cooled, cover pan with foil and refrigerate until just before serving.

6 To serve, reheat chicken over medium heat, stirring often, 3 to 4 minutes, or until hot. Transfer to platter.

White Rice

¹/₄ teaspoon salt
300 g (10 oz) long-grain white rice

1 Bring 750 ml (1¹/₂ pts) water and salt to a boil in medium-size saucepan over high heat.

2 Stir in rice, cover pan, and reduce heat to medium-low. Simmer gently 18 to 20 minutes, or until rice is tender and water is completely absorbed.

3 Fluff rice with fork and transfer to serving dish.